A Gesture of Appreciation to Life

Noor Afasa

BookLeaf Publishing

Presentation by *BookLeaf Publishing*

Web: www.bookleafpub.com

E-mail: info@bookleafpub.com

ISBN: 9789357441629

First edition 2023

To those who make life better,

I appreciate you.

ACKNOWLEDGEMENT

Thank you to all those who have inspired me, and everyone who has been honest and appreciative of my poetry.

Family and friends, thank you for endlessly giving me love and support.

I want to thank Mariyah, Saoirse and Evie - for building my confidence and self-belief. You all inspire me.

I would also like to thank my English (poetry) teacher for her constant encouragement and help on expanding my poetry experiences/ knowledge.

To my best friend, thank you for always listening to me (and letting me drag you to open mics).

And most importantly, thank you Mamma. Thank you for all that you do to make it possible for me to follow my passions. There is no one I appreciate more than you.
I love you.

PREFACE

This book is an insight into my ideas, hopes for the future and general life. From what inspires me, to my family and typical days. A book to open eyes and hearts so that you may realise the beautiful things around you that we all take for granted.

A gesture of appreciation to life.

(Author's note)

This book is my first time writing poetry to be shared on paper and to show others. Although it's quite scary, it's also exciting! I hope that you find my poems relatable and enjoyable, and I hope to continue to learn more and improve my poetry.

perfect picture imperfectly painted

the soft strokes of the brush
promising perfection,
the artist not in a rush.

it started off all beautiful and well
'just like the others'
but, the brush fell
there - ruined perfection.

these accidental 'marks'
a fault in the picture,
the paint permanent on the stomach, the thighs,
the arms.
it lingers.

but, don't stop painting
carry on
when the brush gets wider,
and the curves get bigger
carry on
even if it doesn't 'look like the others',
carry on.
please, make my body perfect
carry on.

and even when you realise that it isn't a pretty
picture,
don't compare me to the others.
put me up with the rest,
show me off and appreciate that i'm different.

don't mistake beauty for imperfection.

be proud of your painting - a masterpiece.
it's the perfect picture imperfectly painted.

beautiful bodies

your body is your home
so why shouldn't you feel comfortable?
each scar carrying a secret or story
and each stretch mark making you more
loveable.

tell yourself how much you love your body -
can't you appreciate all it does?
working so hard to keep us happy and alive
and yet it knows,
how we turn around and feel ashamed of its
"imperfections" and "flaws"
please do share, why do we punish our bodies
over a little weight?
thinking "oh, maybe beauty isn't my fate"

why do we continuously compare and stress?
"if i was skinny, i would wear that dress"
your body doesn't define you or your abilities
doesn't define what me or you can wear
our bodies don't define our beauty

beauty is found everywhere.

flowers

people are like flowers.
forever growing and claiming space.
yet, too afraid
to go beyond what society has given them.

people are like flowers.
from planted, to picked and plucked,
their beauty appreciated - momentarily.
no longer of use, their beauty dried
and colours faded,
they become forgotten, and thrown to a side.

identity

laughter of my bangles
chatter of my jhumke
whispers of my anklets

a Feminist is Me

You see this feminist that speaks in me,
This girl I've silenced for so long?
Now there are these words of hurt,
Upon discovering that it was society who
silenced me all along.

This society that convinced me,
Led me to believe
I shall be nothing but a daughter,
A wife,
A mother,
Because it's society that I must please.

You see this feminist that speaks in me,
This girl I've silenced for so long?
Merely for being a woman
I am silenced and told that I don't belong.
I am made second choice
I am deprived of my voice
I am ignored in the noise
It's because I'm not like the boys.

'Into the kitchen, there you go'
'Cook me something'
What else am I good for?

Because I'm a woman, you think
Do I not have aspirations? No dreams?
Due to our gender difference,
You think you're better than me.

You see this feminist that speaks in me,
This girl I've silenced for so long?
You've been fed all this misogyny,
Stubborn to swallow your pride
That you choke on these views,
And think of yourself so high.

It's not something to be proud of,
This sexism running in your veins.
It's ignorant.
An illness,
Spreading in society.
Sexist minds, sexist brains.

You see this feminist that speaks in me,
This girl I've silenced for so long?
I'm a woman
But tell me, why is that wrong?
Why must you punish me for something I can't
control?

Your mother who birthed you,
Was she not a woman too?

The womb that expanded
And the body that bled,
If not a woman, who else could do that for you?

You see this feminist that speaks in me,
This girl I've silenced for so long?
The silence is gone
My voice is strong
I'm righting the wrong
Let me remind you that I am a woman
And that isn't wrong.

You see,
I am a woman
That can't be defined by society.

A feminist is me.

motherhood

a mother's heart is truly beautiful.
giving and giving,
yet child after child,
they still have more to give.

- selfless

desire

religion is what people follow.
the biggest religion in the world?
desire

Covid

The continuous playing of news in the
background,
Displaying new statistics and figures that have
been found.

Faceless individuals as I walk down another
street,
All of them quick on their feet.

Having places to be,
And people they want to see.

Their frowns and smiles hidden behind a blur of
blue,
More change happening than we knew.

Suddenly everything is forbidden, even the
slightest touch?
It all changed so much.

Schools shut down and instructed to stay at
home,
No one could help but feel alone.

Locked between the same four walls,

"self-isolating
And that was all.

family time

weekends.
all the cousins, aunties and uncles. all the
families come one after another, the house
gradually
getting louder and fuller.
the kids go to play outside, the tea is put to boil
and parents sit
in the living room inside
conversations overlap, words about cars and
children. everyone drinks tea. hours pass. it
starts
to get darker outside and the kids are called in.
everyone sits
together to eat, chaotic with people sat on the
floor and the sofas - food
and drink being passed from one place to
another. something always spills. sometimes,
everyone drinks tea again. and the next weekend
is the same.

Power of Words

It's an escape, I say
A break from reality
A place where I can hide away.

In my head, the words replay
Morphing into a world where I can stay.
A place where my worries aren't my own -
A place like home.

The characters become family and friends
Making it hard to say goodbye when the story
ends.
With each page I turn
There is something new to learn.
And with each chapter read,
There's a new world in my head.

A whole story played out in my head
Showing the power of the words I've read.
All different escapes I've created for myself,
from books once left on a shelf.

home

the grey of the sofas
like the grey of my parents' hair
onions and garlic, and perfume fill up the rooms
refreshing smells of washed clothes
and the strong scent of lemon soap
torn wallpaper
and mascara stains on my mirror
fast footsteps up and down the stairs
busy bustling and shuffling in the kitchen
silencing the shy ticking of the clocks
spices in my mother's curries
freshly squeezed orange juice
and sweet sugar in my sister's baking
my mother's curls
and father's dusty work clothes

my home.

i don't like the rain

i don't like the rain

       i don't like
                hiding
                    behind a coat
and a woolly scarf
i don't like the way the rain

       attacks
               me
how it
                   controls

my mood and plans
i like the freedom
the sun brings me
the hope and positivity
i like breathing
in and looking up to
the expanse of blue
i like running
and feeling the breeze

tears

and then he let a tear slip
it was the trigger
his body caved in
to itself
ashamed
wanting to hide away
i know boys don't cry
he said
but men do
i replied

- toxic masculinity

don't dance

they found her that day
dancing away
hands up in the air
the wind dancing with her hair.
she believed she would be allowed to have fun,
how could she be so dumb?
does she not realise she's a girl
and that they have no place in this world?
that they should be sat down
smile, but don't laugh and never frown
look pretty but not over the top,
and unless instructed to, don't stop.
so they gripped
and kept her down
shoved
their fists into her mouth
to silence any sound
hammered
her knees so she wouldn't stand
pulled
her cheeks and glued them there
said, 'anything but a smile, if you dare'
they told her
'be a girl'
but taught her
'be silent'

healing

wanting something better is like holding a rose,
it hurts at first
so you drop the rose
contemplate on forgetting about it.
don't.
wipe away the blood. lick your wounds.
bandage them.
and then,
pick up your rose again.

a drug

the feeling of a book within your hands
is satisfying
but the smell of the pages
the creativity
is obsessive
a drug.

One day

One day happiness will outweigh sadness
there will be enough food for everyone
sexual assault and rape won't exist
skin colour won't change opinions
gender won't affect one's wage
children won't have to fear financial issues
everyone will care about climate change
the education system will be fair
wars won't be a solution
all cultures will be respected
hopefully
one day.

once a little girl (for my Grandma)

she takes God's name as she stands up,
when she drinks water
and when she sits back down.
amongst chatter and laughter,
and English words
'history' 'happiness' 'she'
she listens - intently.
trying to understand.
her ears, adorned with gold
unable to understand.

her frail brown hands
painted with henna
and their random assuring pats,
light and careful,
yet so strong.
her face has grown tired,
wrinkles and creases - scars of emotions
happiness, tears and worries.
yet, her eyes remain young.
a deep frown, permanently carved.
serious. until she smiles.
and her smile,
the same as in the framed photos.

her eyes - a looking glass.
a look into the past
a past unknown to her grandchildren
a past of a far away land
a land of spices, samosas and sun
a land she brings and keeps in her home, through
her cooking, her accent and her clothes.

and when she thinks,
it's the little girl...
and when she laughs,
it's the little girl...
and when she dreams,
it's the little girl,
in her far away land.

Summer Memories

Memories of
 splashes of green moving
            above and endless blue
     the coolness of icecream on
my tongue offering
            temporary satisfaction.

Memories of
    feeling safe with the front
door open
       family and friends dropping in to say
hi
   along with the occasional green fly.

Memories of
                running around and cycling
        down our backstreet
making friends a happy feeling

Memories of
            warm
  stickiness on our necks
               picking buttercups and making daisy
chains appreciating the beauty of nature

reading

my happy place
lies within pages of books
where i sit
cuddled in blankets
wrapped in darkness
the lights turned off
but light f l i c k e r s from my candles
- a sweet scent
the warmth engulfs me
as do the hidden worlds
hidden beneath the ink
on pages before me
you cannot reach me in
my happy place

www.ingramcontent.com/pod-product-compliance
Lightning Source LLC
La Vergne TN
LVHW021338200726

843509LV00014B/2564